A Book
of Bothersome Cats

written & illustrated by

Janet Kozachek

Finishing Line Press
Georgetown, Kentucky

A Book of Bothersome Cats

Copyright © 2023 by Janet Kozachek
ISBN 979-8-88838-251-6 First Edition
All rights reserved under International and Pan-American Copyright Conventions.
No part of this book may be reproduced in any manner whatsoever without written permission from the publisher, except in the case of brief quotations embodied in critical articles and reviews.

ACKNOWLEDGMENTS

I owe a debt of gratitude to my editors, publishers, family, friends, and many other supporters of this present volume. I would like to thank my husband, Professor Nathaniel Wallace, for appreciating my sardonic wit with such affectionate enthusiasm and support. To my graphic designer, Rachel Bair Ficek, my heartfelt wonder at her presentations of creative designs. To my editor and advisor, JoAngela Edwins, I am grateful for her sage advice and patience. I am flattered and humbled by the support of my friends, in particular Olga Yukhno, for encouraging the inclusion of "just a few more cats." To William Epes and Tamara Miles, many thanks for providing me with a venue for an audience. For the neighborhood cats, I am grateful for their visits and inventive poses around my gardens. I dedicate this book to all.

Publisher: Leah Huete de Maines
Editor: Christen Kincaid
Cover Art: Janet Kozachek
Author Photo: Nathaniel O. Wallace
Cover Design: Rachel Bair Ficek

Order online: www.finishinglinepress.com
also available on amazon.com

Author inquiries and mail orders:
Finishing Line Press
P. O. Box 1626
Georgetown, Kentucky 40324
U. S. A.

Table of Contents

Introduction xi

Cat on a Dark and Rainy Day 1

Muzak Cat 3

Seedy Cat 4

Robot Call Cat 5

Hoarder Cat 7

Techno Cat 9

Nationalist Cat 11

Border Cat 13

Proper Cat 15

Procrastinator Cat 16

Rude Cat 19

Guru Cat 21

Polka Dot Cat 23

Troll Cat 25

Sales Cat 26

Fat Cat 27

Bully Cat 29

Dictator Cat 31

Angry Cat 33

Chemical Cat 35

Conservative Cat 37

Liberal Cat 39

Braggart Cat 41

Jealous Cat 43

Administrator Cat 45

Scatterbrained Cat 46

Factory Cat 47

Compulsive Cat 49

Tell Tale Cat 51

Mispronunciation Cat 53

Conspiracy Cat 55

Cat Lets Some Sun Shine In 57

In memory of Roger Chriss and Gwen Hanks

Introduction

Literature, entertainment, and the media all feature great events and strong emotions—love, grief, despair, and sorrow. The big emotions and the exaltation of grand achievements all figure prominently in both popular and literary culture. But what of the everyday components that may feed into these larger, more formidable aspects of living? *A Book of Bothersome Cats,* through the anthropomorphous central character of Cat, humorously explores daily aggravations and petty annoyances: telephone menus, robot calls, social media trolls, hyperpartisan conversations, accumulations of various kinds of clutter, bullies of all kinds, and censorship. Cat is the unwitting and unwilling recipient of these daily building blocks in his edifice of discontents, made manifest in the characters of other cats that compete for his time. Naming and illustrating them in parody effectively loosens their powerful grip for Cat, as it hopefully will for readers of this book.

The use of animals to portray human foibles is a time-honored tradition that cuts across cultural lines. Why, might a reader ask, should these characteristics be applied to cats? The possible explanation for that would be that these cats are distant enough to enable us to look upon their bothersome aspects from a seemingly safe vantage point. Yet they are familiar enough to be relatable as well. There is research demonstrating that a cat's nervous system has a number of similarities to that of humans. Perhaps there is some unconscious awareness of ourselves in a cat's sense of self-preservation, diffidence, annoyance, and defense of territory—the piteous meow, the hiss, the growl. So too, might we see ourselves wired the same way in our pleasures and devotions—the delight of a coddled, purring feline. As evinced by the plethora of viral cat videos on social media, the popularity of cats endures for the people who see a touch of themselves beneath the claws and fur.

A Book of Bothersome Cats is a sequel to the very popular illustrated book of rhymes, *The Book of Marvelous Cats*, published by **Janet Kozachek** in 2016.

Cat on a Dark and Rainy Day

Cat looks out a window that reaches down to the floor,
just to the left of a patio door.
He swishes his tail as he stares into the yard,
thinking of things that hit his mind hard.
A ruminating Cat is not a good thing,
for he conjures up thoughts that make his brain sting.
Out the window Cat sees a dark cloud rolling in.
It makes him think of a cat who always wanted to win.
The cloud lets loose the rain, and Cat starts to pout.
He growls to himself, for he cannot go out.
He thinks of a cat who did him a wrong,
others who were weak, but one who was strong.
There was that big calico bully on the corner of Main,
and that competitor cat who would drive him insane.
There was a Tabby cat that was too tight with his money,
and his brother who thought his stupid flea jokes were funny.
His alley cat friend frequented disreputable places.
His uncle shorthair greeted him with strange faces.
Cat's brother-in-law would not invite him to stay,
for his house was stuffed up because he threw nothing away.
But his aunt was much worse, Cat thought with dismay,
for she counted every mouse twice and vacuumed ten times a day.
Cat's daughter was too liberal indeed for his taste
—recycling even her mouse tails so they would not go to waste.
There was that stranger cat in the corner café
who talked too loudly about the day she was spayed.
Cat learned her life story, like it or not,
because he had paid for his meal and was glued to his spot.
Cat stared outside at the now pouring down rain
and thought of more cats that had caused him much pain.
His cousin the braggart's daily catch of rodent fare
were ten times, he claimed, what Cat could hunt down in a year.
When Cat was at work, an angry colleague would spit
and jump up and down, always throwing a fit.
Cat did not like him, not at all, not one bit.
Cat's sister had kittens of whom she was proud,
but she always let them sing too long, hard and loud.
They disturbed uncle Cat and gave him a headache

that was resistant to anything Cat attempted to take. It just seemed that other cats were eagerly employed in making Cat on a dark day feel alone and annoyed. Until the day brightens and the sun starts to shine, Cat's thoughts will be filled with these awful felines.

Muzak Cat

Muzak Cat meows and howls all day.
People wish he'd go away.
He sings to them in elevators,
in department stores, on escalators.
You'll hear him in the shower, when washing your hair.
His catophonic sounds are everywhere.
When Muzak Cat feels that he is bored,
he'll growl into a phone, and then press "record."
That insipid tune playing when you're on "hold"
that you put on speaker, when you've laundry to fold,
that hums in your brain like a bothersome gnat?
It was Muzak Cat that composed all that.
He puts the buzz in your car when you back up too far,
the ring in your door when pressing pedal to the floor.
He'll write predictable jingles all saccharine and cloying.
Muzak Cat is the king of all tunes annoying.
He sings, he bops, he scats and pings.
He'll write a sickening tune to anything.

Seedy Cat

Seedy Cat wears a salacious grin
on account of where he's been.
He frequents the most questionable places
and lingers long in seedy spaces.
Every time he disappears for a while,
he'll eventually be found in Red Light Mile.
Oh the things he'll do there cannot be mentioned
—even by the well intentioned.
Can he be helped? Can he be saved?
Most likely not—he's too depraved!

Robot Call Cat

Robot Call Cat calls when you're at rest or at labor,
pretending that he might be your next door neighbor.
He addresses you by your first name but not by your last
to fool you into believing that he's a good friend from your past.
Do you have all the collars you need to ward off every flea?
Would you buy one if it comes with an extended warranty?
Should you donate to Robot Cat's worthy cause?
How much cash can you spare for his grasping paws?
When you're tired or weary or worn out to the bone,
that's when he's most likely to telephone.
He'll call when you reach the top of a ladder
or when you need to attend to a very full bladder.
With a meow that's mechanical, neither rising nor falling,
he'll find you all day long, and he'll just keep on calling.

Hoarder Cat

Hoarder cat collects and keeps everything.
To old toys and used prey he'll tenaciously cling.
Hoarder cat keeps other cats' discarded mice.
He stores ten thousand in his cellar—even those with lice.
He keeps boxes of lizards inherited from his mother
and has closets full of moths handed down from his brother.
Hoarder cat has bargain flea collars crammed into a shed.
What doesn't fit in there he stuffs under his bed.
He stores a few hundred rat traps tied up in a sack.
The neighbors who lent them will not get them back.
Hoarder Cat saves every stink bug that lands on his casement
and keeps them in a moldy carpet downstairs in his basement.
He collects pet rocks and broken clocks
and boxes upon boxes of worn out odd socks.
Hoarder Cat has an enormous collection of stuff.
His friends always tell him that it is more than enough.
"There will be no room for yourself," they implore, "if you keep every mouse."
Hoarder Cat just smiles and exclaims, "Then I'll buy a bigger house!"

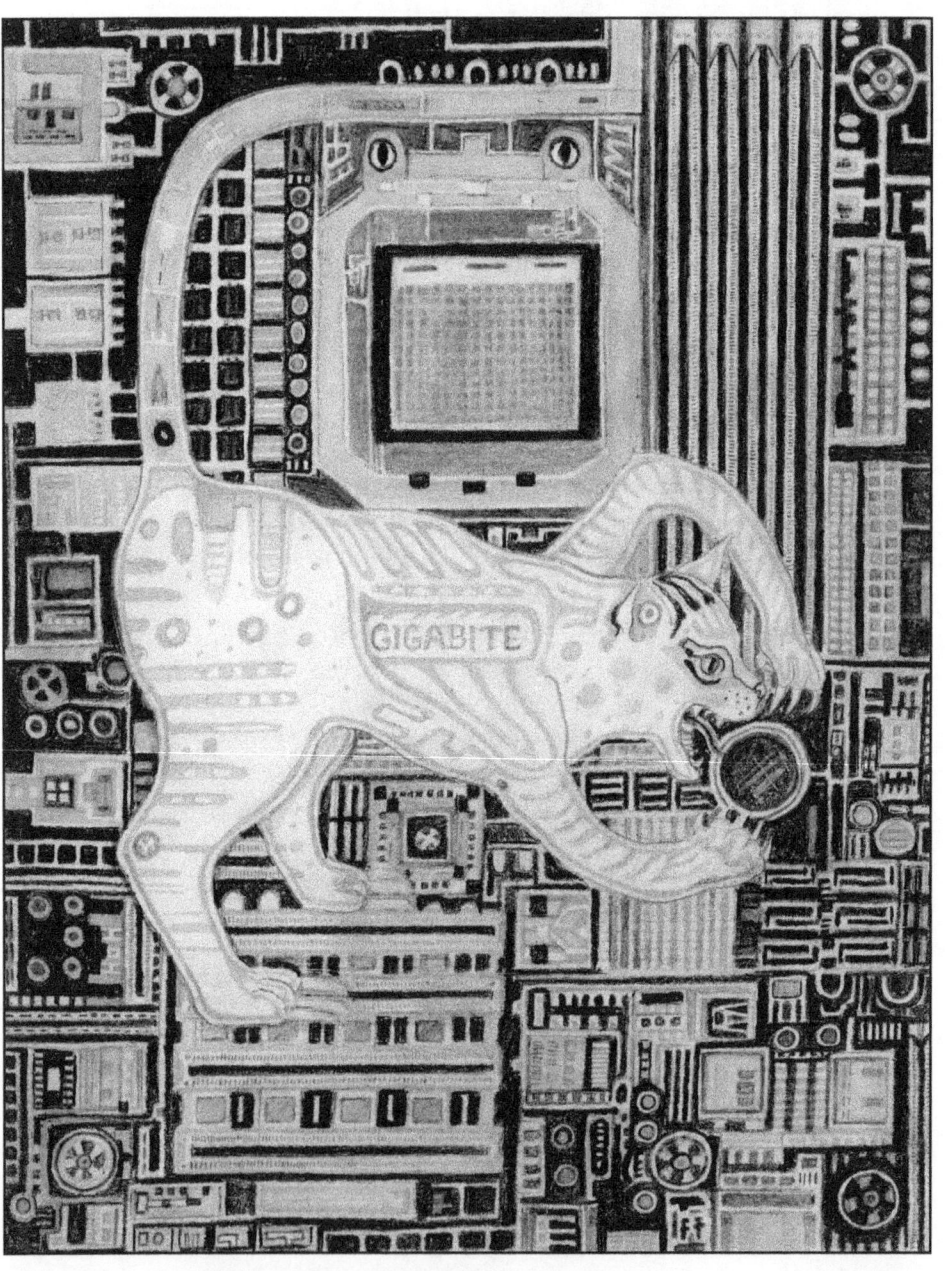

Techno Cat

Techno Cat is at the head of his pack.
He slides his paws up a keyboard,
then down again and back.
He'll look at your house
then pass it on by
if accommodations do not include some Wi-fi.
Techno Cat will supply his own mouse,
although he might take a mega bite out.
Every question he asks has no in between.
It is yes or no on a binary screen.
He stores all your data and makes a good penny
selling your searches, purchases, and comments to many.

Nationalist Cat

Nationalist Cat hoists a flag up his tail.
He thinks that all foreign cats should be put into jail.
He keeps his litter box clean, and his country pristine,
allowing no entry to cats with paws not stamped green.
Nationalist Cat is authentically, genetically purebred.
He is pure Catastonian, from his toes to his head.
Nationalist Cat is fond of executive orders
to keep unfavorable cats away from his borders.
But if his national population should begin to tailspin
Nationalist Cat might just let a few outsiders in.

Border Cat

Border Cat sits on top of a wall.
He pretends not to listen when others call.
He thinks it a proper dividing line
between good guy cats and not the best felines.
They don't deserve his crunchy treats
—the ones that he alone earns and eats.
He swears he'll never let them in,
because Nationalist Cat is his next of kin.

Proper Cat

Proper Cat sits pretty and prissy,
having tea and scones with an appropriate missy.
He wears a tie at the table and dons little white gloves
and a kitty top hat that his mistress just loves.
Mistress' house is well ordered, cleaned spic and span.
There is no smell at all from her garbage can.
She does not lean forward at the table or make a backwards bend,
and the paintings on her walls will never offend.
This is just the right home for a Proper Cat,
he thinks as he tips his little black hat.

Proper Cat always knows where to begin
in order to avoid showing too much skin.
On top of his head his black top hat
is hand tailored to fit a gentleman cat.
His bow tie sits underneath his jaws,
and little white gloves cover both his paws.
He sits with good posture in his tux at the table.
He musters all the restraint that a cat is able,
when his mistress, thoroughly buttoned and zipped,
serves him petits fours mice in frosting dipped.
If mistress eats a pickle he knows not to look.
Proper Cat will hide in his discreet dark nook.

When mistress puts a banana to her mouth,
Proper Cat discreetly pulls the window shades south.
He'll hang wildlife photography upon her walls,
tipping right then left with his little gloved paws.
Proper cat loves the birds, the lizards and bees,
when they fly around flowers and flit around trees.
He likes their innocent lack of reason
—as long as it's not their mating season.
Proper Cat knows the rules of social media
and never posts pictures that others might find seedia.

Procrastinator Cat

Procrastinator Cat tends to put things off.
When he says he'll get the job done, other cats just scoff.
He delays raking the leaves from his back yard,
then complains that the weeds now make it too hard.

His back porch needs repair and he has knots in his hair.
There is a hole in his litter box, but he doesn't care.
His bills pile up on his kitchen table.
He'll get to them some time, when he is able.

There's an old rusted cat carrier that's been there for years,
along with an assortment of motorcycle gears.
"I'll pick them up tomorrow," he promises the neighbors.
They'll be there some more decades with no show of his labors.

He puts things off, the procrastinator cat.
He has an attention span as short as a gnat.
Even though it makes him grow substantially thinner,
he delays catching essential mice for his dinner.

Procrastinator Cat has other things on his plate,
and he always makes lunch just a little too late.
He tells family and friends that he is not a waiter.
They can start eating without him, he'll get to them later.

He has half-done projects everywhere on display.
He'll finish them up when he gets to them some day.
He starts one thing, then this and then that,
never finishing anything, for he's a procrastinator cat.

His wife tells him, "Stay put and complete at least one thing."
"I cannot," he tells her, because the light has grown dim.
You can yell, you can beg, and sometimes shout,
but this cat will stop working when it gets too cold out.

When others stay on task, and glued to a spot.
Procrastinator cat will quit when the weather is hot.
He looks in the mirror and sees nothing off,

claiming to never have heard of Oblomov.
But don't call him lazy, not industrious or such.
Sometimes he just takes on a little too much.

Rude Cat

When you opine, Rude Cat interrupts you,
to tell you his smarter point of view.
Rude Cat does not like your taste in holiday art.
When you decorate your tree, he'll tear it apart.
Put on a few pounds and he'll call you fat
and scowl at your child and call her a brat.
When you sit by his side, expecting a mew
Rude Cat can't restrain a belch or two.
He'll ask the same question multiple times.
When you try to answer, out the window he climbs.
As you go out the door in your Sunday best,
he'll laugh at your shoes and smirk at your vest.
Because he delights in being a Rude Cat,
he'll snarl when he asks if you're going out dressed like *that*.
Rude Cat points out the small stains on your pants.
He'll insist that you remove them, because he knows that you can't.
Rude Cat will occupy the bathroom that you need to use,
by taking a three hour bath and a toy boat cruise.
He won't speak to you when he joins you for dinner,
except to say that you ought to be thinner!
He'll gobble down sweets, treats, meats and such
all the while telling you that you're eating too much!
If you bring him a gift, he'll say its too cheap
and that your pockets don't appear to be very deep.
When you get old, Rude Cat will note that you're wrinkly,
pointing out your thinning hair, patched teeth, and your parts that are crinkly.
But one day when you are no longer sitting where you sat,
he might be sorry that he was such a Rude Cat.

Guru Cat

Guru Cat puts your mind at ease
for just a modest fee, if you please.
Take the Cat's advice!
You'll get job offers
—just as long as you fill his very own coffers.
Guru Cat will grant your every wish,
if you'll buy him lifetime servings of tuna fish.
Guru Cat will set your soul on fire.
His affirmations and proclamations do inspire.
Get out of yourself!
Climb out of your ditch!
Stroke the Guru Cat's tail, and you'll find yourself rich!
Throw dollars his way, and you'll be okay.
Pay homage to Guru Cat, starting today!
He'll promise that all of your days will be sunny,
purring so sweetly when you show him your money.

Polka Dot Cat

Some cats like stripes, others like dots.
This cat sports only polka dots.
Her dress may be Polish or it might be Czech.
She only knows that it makes her dance a half step.
When in her dress of polka dots,
her smile lights up like a thousand watts.
She lets her hair down and combs out the knots
as she swirls in her dress of polka dots.
She swishes her tail and out she trots
in a phantasmagoria of polka dots.
Her dress might be Czech or it could be Polish.
When she wears it at her laptop it makes her Trollish.
And although Polka Dot Cat claims that she is not,
she is sometimes mistaken for a Russian Bot.
Polka Dot Cat eats only cream that clots
while dressed up in her polka dots.
She wears her spotty dress to parties in Spain,
although her DNA test says she's from Ukraine.
Polka Dot Cat claims that it is a psychomachia
to be thought Slovenian but be from Slovakia.
She puts all her relatives in their proper slots,
that silly little cat dressed in polka dots.
They could be Polish, but they might be Czech
But they're all related so what the heck!

Troll Cat

Troll Cat follows you on social media,
denigrating all your links to Kittypedia.
He tells you that he thinks it strange,
for a cat to say that people can cause the climate to change.
Then quick as a wink, off he'll tread,
and perch himself on another's thread.
His whiskers twitch and he begins to smirk,
as he calls a climate change denier cat a "jerk."
He finds it amusing to be a troll,
gallivanting about from pole to pole,
poking one friend, then prodding another,
confessing to a sister, then tattling to her brother.
Troll cat sparks fires by calling out names,
keeping the taunts ever flowing to fan all the flames.
Pretending to be a Persian Cat he calls a Siamese weird,
suggesting he hide his face by growing a beard.
Then he says Siamese Cats are the best cats around
and that the Maine Coon Cats have put on too many pounds.
Just to add to Troll Cat's fun for a while,
He steals the famous Lola Angora Cat's profile.
Through this illustrious cat's face he speaks,
spreading news that a Tom Cat cannot control his leaks.
Then pretending to be an educated Tabby,
He says that Norwegian Forest Cats tend to be too flabby.
Then Troll Cat summons everyone to say
that the only good cats left are all from Norway.
Troll Cat just enjoys stirring up all kinds of trouble
—especially for folks who live in a bubble.
He can do it all from inside his house,
for he rules the world with a keyboard and mouse.

Sales Cat

Sales cat will serve you with a steady hand,
and help you find your particular brand.
He'll ensure you'll be the toast of your neighborhood,
when you purchase his special big bag of goods:
a widget for your whiskers and a gadget for your paws.
He sells wax to prevent blisters and plated clippers for your claws.
A successful feline hunter has a scheme that's smart.
Everything is outlined clearly in his compartment chart.
Sales Cat will explain and then train you later
on how to tell your life story in an elevator.
For that mousing job that requires an interview,
give a confident meow, he advises, but not a meek mew.
Whether you are cat or if you are a man,
Sales Cat will give you a ready-made plan.

Fat Cat

Fat Cat smokes a large cigar
and drives a big gas guzzling car.
He sleeps on a mattress stuffed full of money
and sets some on fire because he thinks it funny.
When asked to move on, he just stays put.
Fat Cat will not budge, and he'll bite your foot.
He rules where he sits from his powerful spot.
He won't be replaced—no he will not.
Fat Cat will sit there forever, in light and in dark,
for he is a wined and dined feline oligarch.

Bully Cat

Bully Cat intimidates all the others,
warning them not to complain to their mothers.
He is a big, loud, pudgy-pawed, domineering feline.
To the weak and unprotected he makes a bee line.
He flexes his muscles and thumps his hard belly,
making all the other cats feel much too smelly.
He then gives his strong, hard belly a pat,
and makes all the other cats feel far too fat.
Kitty toadies surround him in tightly knit gangs,
hissing and growling and showing their fangs.
They make all the other cats tremble in fear.
But when they abandon Bully Cat, he sheds a small tear.

Dictator Cat

Dictator Cat can be seen from afar
riding in the back of his big black car.
Dressed in shiny boots the color of tar,
he thinks that he's back in the USSR.
He's lord of all the cat countries he sees
—his territory marked by wherever he pees.
Dictator Cat keeps his minions in a bind,
because he owns them all; soul, body and mind.
Any calls for autonomy don't make much of a dent,
for he brooks no opposition and no dissent.
Over much of the earth he seeks dominion,
despite civil rights and world opinion.
He sits at the end of a very long table
so his comrades can't tell that he's most unstable.

Angry Cat

Angry Cat's face always turns bright red
as blood vessels pop out all over his head.
If he makes a mistake, it is not okay
if a hint of criticism should come his way.
He'll puff himself out and gnash his teeth
if any other cat would give him such grief.

Angry Cat never picks up his trash.
When asked to do so, his tongue will lash.
Other cats shy away; he can be awfully rough,
and not too accommodating when protecting his stuff.

Angry Cat is a very busy kitty.
He sits at the head of every committee.
He wants to have perks, though neglecting his work.
To those who deny him, he'll become very curt.

Angry Cat leaves behind his wifely feline.
To his mistress puss he'll be more kind.
Mistress puss does his work as he hems and haws,
then hangs his head out a window to make Cat calls.

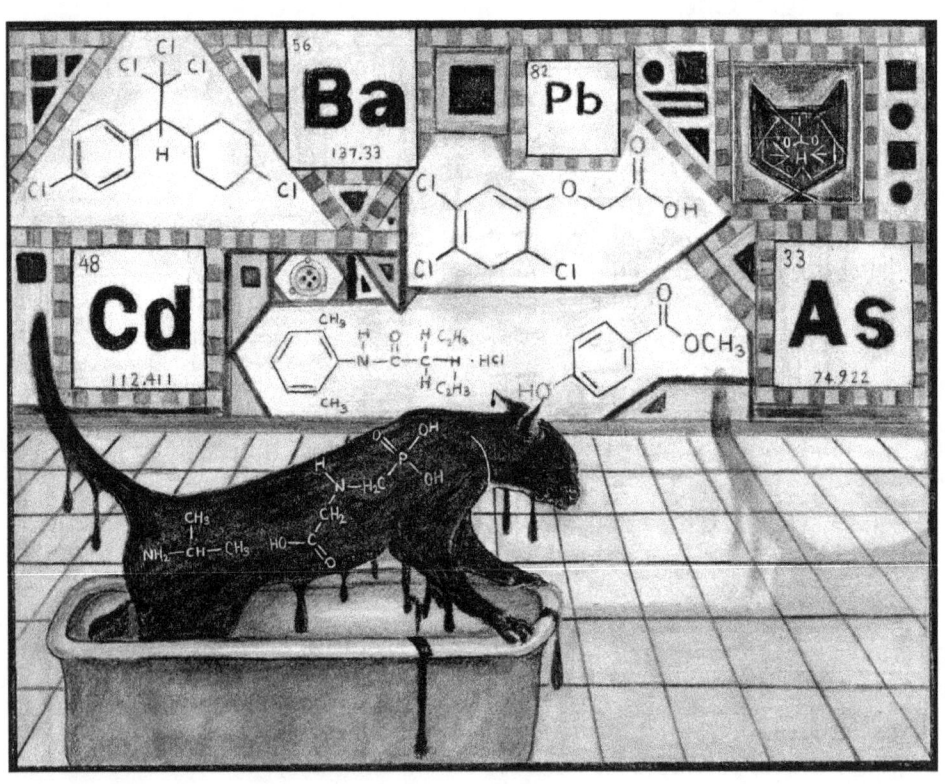

Chemical Cat

Chemical Cat
climbs out of a vat,
dripping waste products
onto the floor mat.
Drug products, pesticides and radioactive slime
—he doesn't consider any of it to be a crime.
Chemical Cat gives his products great adulation,
and is a very big fan of deregulation.
Why bother chasing mice and getting agitated
when it would be easier to just have them all fumigated?
The chemical solution, he thinks, is the perfect thing.
Chemical Cat even wears a benzene ring.

Conservative Cat

Conservative Cat wears a suit and bow tie.
He watches Fox News while eating fish fry.
He tips his room service with no more than a pittance
and doesn't believe in free lunches for kittens.

Liberal Cat

Liberal Cat listens to NPR
while driving her fuel-efficient mini car.
She promotes her causes to great effect
and only has friends who are politically correct.

Braggart Cat

Braggart Cat is full of hot air.
He finds lesser cats with whom to compare
—the ones with hair not sufficiently curly,
who worked too hard and left school early.
He laughs at the kitties who live in small houses
and who can only chase down the littlest mouses.
He struts across his yard with a deliberate swagger,
satisfied in himself because he's a bragger.
He lets all the cats know how long his tail is,
and that he's an artist, a musician and a great math whiz.
Braggart cat is muscular, fit and trim.
He says that all the lady cats just adore him.
He earns much by his hunting and gets his taxes done early.
His teeth are whiter than other cats—in fact they are pearly.

Braggart cat makes fun of cats who buy the cheaper cat food.
He eats salmon with caviar when he's in the mood.
He displays his awards in a prominent place,
making certain his Mewlitzer is in front of your face.
When his prizes are mentioned, he pretends to be shy,
by saying "I'm humbled, I'm honored," and "I could just cry."
Only the best roses grow on Braggart Cat's trellis,
and he delights in making the other cats jealous.

Jealous Cat

Jealous cat gets very red in the face
when a competitor cat takes over his place.
His paws go cold and his neck turns hot
when a usurper cat sits in his spot.
Jealous cat makes noises like a cat who is haunted
when another cat gets what Jealous Cat wanted.
When his friends and relatives buy anything new,
he immediately wants the very same thing too.
He feels scorned and burned by what other cats earned
and rues this life when it appears never his turn.
Jealous Cat doesn't like it—how thwarted he feels
when he sees cats going places, while he's just spinning his wheels.
Other cats catch mice that fill up their tables
when Jealous Cat seems pathetically unable.
Braggart Cat's plate of mice overflowing when he's far from done,
has Jealous Cat fuming because he could only catch one.
When Braggart Cat boasts that he can win anything with little travail,
he hopes Braggart Cat's teeth fall out and that he'll trip on his tail.

Administrator Cat

Administrator Cat sits at a desk all day,
taking one out of a hundred phone calls that come his way.
He looks up a few records when he has a mind to,
then he does what all the other Bureau Cats do
—give a slice of advice looking grim and sage,
then spends the rest of his time on his profile page.
He puts in an appearance every now and then,
sending thoughts and prayers, then joining the "Amen."
When his constituents cry that their kittens will die,
he gives them a phone menu with a recorded reply.
He puts on a fine hat, saying "I'll look into that."
"We'll study the problem, and then we'll get back."

Scatterbrained Cat

The Scatterbrained cat eats as fast as he can,
then forgets what he did with the cat food can.
All at once he hunts lizards, mice and moles
—not one at a time, for he has no control.
Scatterbrained cat changes the subject many times
whenever he gets on the phone or goes online.
He tries to listen to Puss and Boots on tape,
but before the end, he is snoring, his mouth agape.

Scatterbrained cat always loses his keys
—it makes him scratch his head along with his fleas.
He finally finds them about two weeks later,
buried down deep in a litter box crater.
He tries to clean out his oven and gets covered with soot.
He would have worn gloves, if he knew where they were put.
He misplaces his glasses, then has a small fall.
What time are his memory classes? He cannot recall.

Factory Cat

Factory Cat works on an assembly line
making toys and treats for the discerning feline.
He stuffs some catnip into a toy mouse locket,
then squirrels some away into his own back pocket.
"It's a dog eat dog world, and every cat for himself,"
he says as he filches items from off of a shelf.
Factory Cat tells us that the powers that be
don't work for you, him, her or me.
"Those in control will not give a just due,
so if they give you one thing be sure to take two."
Factory Cat has his own rules and ignores any ban.
He gets what he can, from feline or man.

Compulsive Cat

Compulsive Cat vacuums all day long,
picking up debris with the use of a tong.
She won't put her paw on a garbage pail,
so instead she opens it with a flick of her tail.
She gives every box of kitty crackers its own special tag,
and each mouse she hunts up has its own zippy bag.
Every mouse is measured from his tail to his nose,
then arranged from large to small in long, neat rows.
Compulsive Cat wraps up her lizards in plastic,
then binds them up with hypoallergenic elastic.
Only the best birds from her clean yard are chosen,
steam cooked with potatoes then packed up and frozen.
She spoons them into tupperware bowls, sealing the lid with a pop,
then carefully pens month, date, year, time, and weight in ink on the top.

Tell-Tale Cat

A long-haired cat sits in a corner café.
She has an audience and a lot to say.
While the other cats are busy eating hors d'oeuvres,
she sits admiring her own voluptuous curves.
She tells her friends how she got them by eating just right
and how her weight is now appropriate for her particular height.
Tell-Tale cat explains to her captive audience cats,
how she used to believe that she was overly fat.
She tells them in a voice that the whole eatery hears,
how a therapist helped her overcome her fat fears.
Tell-Tale Cat has more to say in a voice piercing and loud
for every cat far and near in the corner café crowd.
No subject is too private or at all off the table.
She'll talk most of the night, whenever she's able:
the dreaded details of the day she was spayed,
the estranged mother cat who then came to her aid,
the fleas that infested her not one time but many,
and the worm pills that cost her a pretty good penny.
Nothing is too personal, too uncouth or too gory,
and the entire café now knows her life story.

Mispronunciation Cat

Mispronunciation Cat works as a media announcer.
Before that, he was a bar stool bouncer.
There are things foreign to him, that he knows nothing about.
But he says whatever he pleases and doesn't bother to find out.
He describes the capital of China like a French greeting
—not with a "j" as in "jump" but a sound soft and fleeting.
The capital of Russia, he is so inclined,
to pronounce as if it includes a bovine.
Igbo, for the earnest student, has a soft "g."
But this cat thinks that it rhymes with "dig bow" if you please.
He'll say "Wang" like a "bang," instead of a bong,
and no one will correct him, or tell him he's wrong.
Mispronunciation Cat thinks Worcester should not sound like a rooster,
and instead calls it as he sees it so that it sounds like "poor jester."
Mispronunciation Cat knows what names are if you live in the west,
but cats of the east, north, and south know how to say their names best.
They implore him with vociferous and hearty endeavor,
but Mispronunciation Cat still says their names just "however."
If this poor Cat should ever open a door to a war,
then he may not know how to say what he's fighting for.

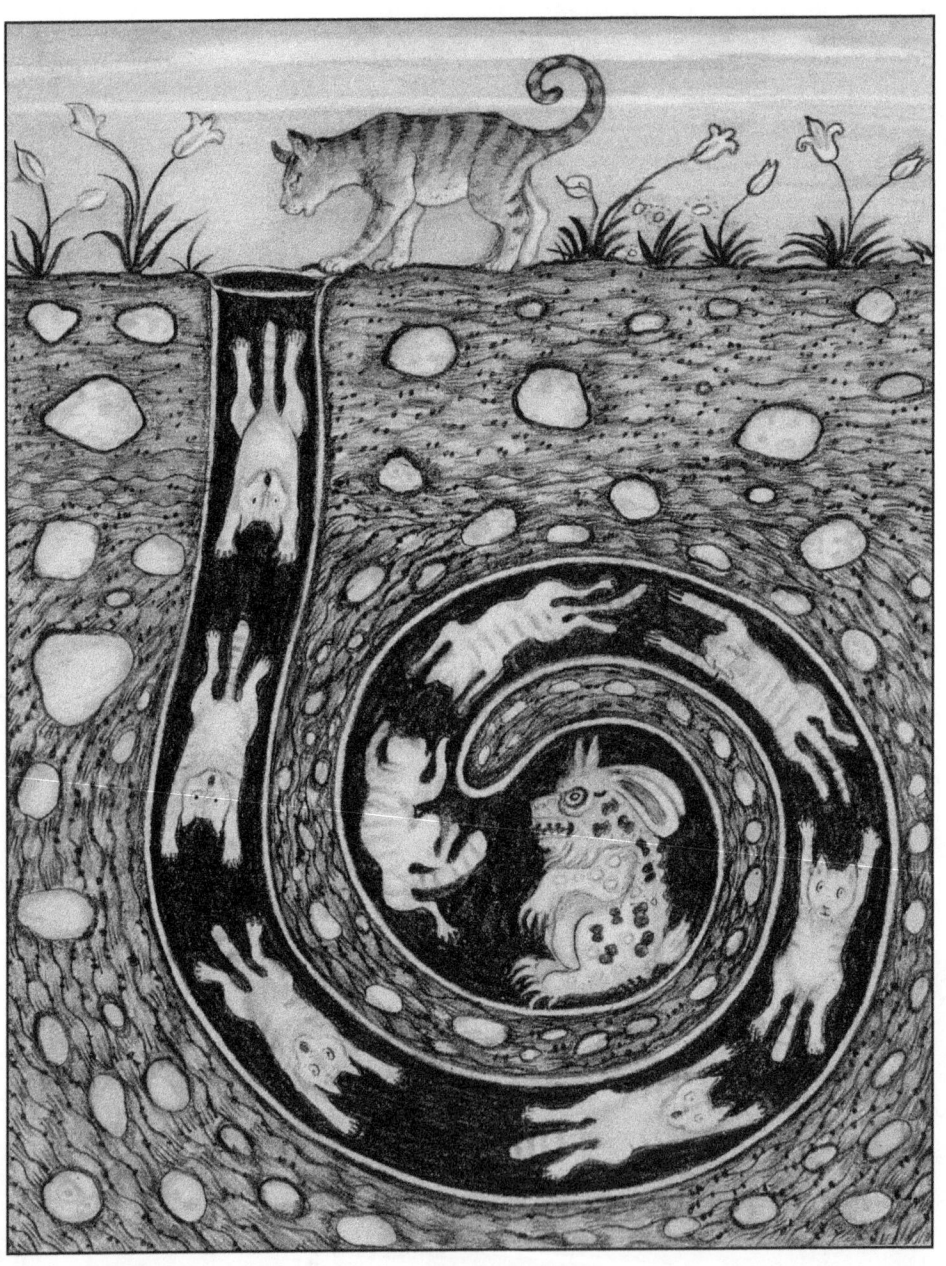

Conspiracy Cat

Conspiracy Cat dives down rabbit holes,
finding explanations for all his woes.
He does not notice facts askew
nor information not peer reviewed.
When his fellows notice he has neither reason nor rhyme,
he retorts that his journeys took up much of his time.
From where he sits up high upon his perch,
rabbit holes look more like informed research.
His friends advise him to stick to the mainstream media
and to consult reputable journals and an encyclopedia.
Conspiracy Cat waves them all away like annoying gnats.
"Why read the papers," he says," when there are better pod cats?"

Cat Lets Some Sun Shine In

Dark clouds scatter and the sun shines through.
Silver-winged doves begin to coo.
The rain slows to a drizzle, then comes to a stop.
Cat flicks his ears back and forth and makes his tail flip-flop.
As Cat sits bathed in the sunlight, his fur turns warm.
His shadows are behind him, and so is the storm.
The day is young yet, with prey to be caught.
Cat reflected to himself upon what that storm had brought.
All those bothersome cats dispersed along with rain clouds
—those kitties with bad habits and ones that howled too loud.
Cat smiled to himself, his eyes half closed.
He purred contentedly and twitched his pink nose.
Despite those cats who annoyed me, there's no need to be gruff.
In the end they're no more to me than pieces of fluff.
The cat who always insufferably nags
may very well be wed to the Tom cat who brags.
A waste of precious time it would be to cajole and implore them.
Better to rest at ease with oneself and simply ignore them.
Bully cat may be large and appear to rule,
but his circle of friends is in fact minuscule.
The cat who talks too loudly in a restaurant,
makes herself too available, inviting others to taunt.
The cat who surrounded himself with the stuff that he hoards,
would not have done so unless he were bored.
Best to refrain with some cats from prodding and poking.
Political cats cannot tolerate joking.
Cat let all the other cats go, the ones who caused him such grief.
Then he let out a generous feline sigh of relief.
He coughed to himself and gave a sly huff.
Why bother in the affairs of such small stuff?
In the end Cat knew that when he gets annoyed,
that there are some cats to ignore and some to avoid.

Janet Kozachek hails from Princeton Junction, New Jersey, where her rural formative years were spent drawing and writing in nature. Her subsequent education was unusually eclectic, having traveled, worked and studied in Europe, China and the United States. She obtained her Master of Fine Arts Degree in Drawing and Painting from Parsons School of Design in New York, where she also studied poetry with J.D. McClatchy. Her Certificate of Graduate Study in Chinese Art from the Central Academy of Fine Art (CAFA) in the People's Republic of China included the study of Chinese poetry and painting. Her undergraduate study at Rutgers was in science (biology) and art.

In addition to her painting, Janet Kozachek is a well-known mosaic artist, and was the Founding President of the Society of American Mosaic Artists. Her work is in a number of museums and private collections, and she was the recipient of the award for excellence in drawing from Art Fields (2019), a Puffin Foundation Award, National Endowment for the Arts awards, a Heritage Foundation Award, and a Humanities Council Award. Her poetry and illustrations have been published in *Undefined* magazine, the journal *Ekphrasis,* and *Local Life.* Ms. Kozachek is the author of *The Book of Marvelous Cats, My Women, My Monsters,* and *A Rendering of Soliloquies— Figures Painted in Spots of Time.* Janet Kozachek was the recipient of the 2020 Common Ground on the Hill Award for Excellence in the Traditional Arts.

When not writing, drawing, or painting in her studio in Orangeburg, South Carolina, Janet Kozachek finds joy in cooking, gardening, and making ceramic musical instruments. Her work can be found in the Artisans Center in Walterboro, South Carolina.
www.janetkozachek.net
kozachekart.blogspot.com
kozachek@bellsouth.net

www.ingramcontent.com/pod-product-compliance
Lightning Source LLC
Chambersburg PA
CBHW031127160426
43192CB00008B/1134